P9-BII-044

ROTIS & SUBZIS

Tarla Dalal

SANJAY & CO.
BOMBAY

Tenth Printing : 2001

Price Rs. 185/-

Published & Distributed by : **Sanjay & Company,**
353, A-1, Shah & Nahar Industrial Estate, Dhanraj Mill Compound,
Lower Parel (W), Mumbai - 400 013. INDIA.
Tel. : (91-22) 496 8068 Fax : (91-22) 496 5876 E-mail : sanjay@tarladalal.com

Printed by : **Jupiter Prints,** Mumbai

: Designed by :
Niranjan Kamatkar

: Photographs by :
Vinay Mahidhar

OTHER BOOKS BY TARALA DALAL

WESTERN COOKING
The Complete Italian Cook Book
The Chocolate Cook Book
Eggless Desserts
Mocktails & Snacks
Soups & Salads
Mexican Cooking
Easy Gourmet Cooking

INDIAN COOKING
Tava Cooking
Desi Khana
The Complete Gujarati Cook Book
Mithai
Chaat
Achaar aur Parathe

HEALTH COOKING
Low Calorie Healthy Cooking
Eat Your Way to Good Health
Pregnancy Cook Book

EASTERN COOKING
Chinese Cooking
Thai Cooking
Baby and Toddler Cook Book

GENERAL COOKING
Exciting Vegetarian Cooking
Party Cooking
Microwave Cooking
Quick & Easy Vegetarian Cooking
Saatvik Khana
Mixer Cook Book
Pleasures of Vegetarian Cooking
Delights of Vegetarian Cooking
Joys of Vegetarian Cooking
Cooking With Kids
Snacks Under Ten Minutes

MINI SERIES
A New World of Idlis & Dosas
Pizzas and Pasta
Microwave Desi Khana
Cooking under 10 Minutes
Roz Ka Khana
T. V. Meals

ISBN No. 81-86469-06-0

Visit us on our Home Page http://www.tarladalal.com

CONTENTS

ROTIS

PRESSURE COOKER ROTIS

TOASTED ROTIS

TAVA ROTIS

FRIED ROTIS

SUBZIS

PUNJABI AND MOGHLAI STYLE

CURRIES AND KOFTAS

WESTERN TOUCH

PROVINCIAL STYLE

BASIC RECIPES

INTRODUCTION

In this book, I have incorporated different ways of making rotis e.g. rotis in a toaster and naans in a pressure cooker! Surprise your guests by serving naans made without a tandoor.

As regards subzis, you will find Punjabi and Moghlai style subzis, curries and koftas as also vegetables with a Western touch and vegetables from other parts of India. I have tried to avoid rich vegetables and instead given recipes with a light and healthy touch.

In the basic recipes, I have included four useful gravies.

Wishing you happy eating,

Tarla Dalal

PRESSURE COOKER NAAN

Now you can make naan in your pressure cooker. You don't need a tandoor.

PREPARATION TIME: 30 MINUTES. COOKING TIME: 10 MINUTES. MAKES 20 NAANS.

500 grams plain flour (maida)
$1^1/_2$ teaspoons sugar
20 grams fresh yeast or 2 teaspoons dry yeast
2 tablespoons fresh curds
25 grams ghee or margarine or butter
1 teaspoon salt

1. Sieve the flour very well.
2. Mix the sugar and yeast in 1 teacup of warm water and stir unti the yeast dissolves. Cover and wait for 5 to 7 minutes until the mixture is full of froth.
3. Add this liquid along with the curds, ghee and salt to the flour and make a soft dough by adding some more warm water.
4. Knead the dough for at least 6 to 7 minutes.
5. Keep the dough under a wet cloth for 30 minutes.
6. Knead again for 1 minute.
7. Divide the dough into 20 small pieces and shape into naans.
8. Grease a pressure cooker very lightly with oil. Remove the lid from the pressure cooker and heat it upside down.
9. Take each naan, apply a little water on one side and stick the wet side around the inside of the pressure cooker till brown spots appear. You can apply 3 to 4 naans at a time inside the walls of a pressure cooker.
10. Remove and apply butter.

⇛ **Serve hot.**

MASALA PANEER NAAN

PICTURE ON PAGE 35

A very popular naan.

PREPARATION TIME: 30 MINUTES. COOKING TIME: 10 MINUTES. MAKES 20 NAANS.

For the dough

500 grams plain flour (maida)
$1\frac{1}{2}$ teaspoons sugar
20 grams fresh yeast or 2 teaspoons dry yeast
2 tablespoons fresh curds
25 grams ghee or margarine or butter
1 teaspoon salt

For the stuffing

100 grams grated paneer, page 72
1 onion, chopped
3 to 4 chopped green chillies
2 tablespoons chopped coriander
salt to taste

1. Sieve the flour very well.
2. Mix the sugar and yeast in 1 teacup of warm water and stir until the yeast dissolves. Cover and wait for 5 to 7 minutes until the mixture is full of froth.
3. Add this liquid along with the curds, ghee and salt to the flour and make a soft dough by adding some more warm water.
4. Knead the dough for at least 6 to 7 minutes.
5. Keep the dough under a wet cloth for 30 minutes.
6. Knead again for 1 minute.
7. Mix the ingredients for the stuffing well.
8. Divide the dough into 20 small balls, flatten into naans and put 1 teaspoon of the filling in the centre.
9. Close the edges and roll into oblong shape or any other shape you like.
10. Grease a pressure cooker very lighly with oil. Remove the lid from the pressure cooker and heat the cooker upside down.
11. Take each naan, apply a little water on one side and stick the wet side around the inside of the pressure cooker till brown spots appear. You can apply 3 to 4 naans at a time inside the walls of a pressure cooker.
12. Remove and apply butter.

⇛ **Serve hot.**

MISI ROTI

A famous Rajasthan roti.

PREPARATION TIME: 10 MINUTES. COOKING TIME: 30 MINUTES. MAKES 20 ROTIS.

2 teacups gram flour (besan)
1 teacup plain flour (maida)
1 teacup wheat flour (gehun ka atta)
1 onion, finely chopped
2 to 3 green chillies, chopped
1 teaspoon ajwain
2 tablespoons chopped coriander or fenugreek (methi) leaves
4 tablespoons ghee
salt to taste

1. Mix together all the ingredients with enough water and make a semi-stiff dough.
2. Knead the dough well and keep for $^1/_2$ hour. Knead again.
3. Roll out into thin rounds and cook them either in a pressure cooker or on a tava with a little ghee.
   Serve hot with butter or ghee.

Pressure cooker method

1. Grease a pressure cooker very lightly with oil. Remove the lid from the pressure cooker and heat the cooker upside down.
2. Take each naan, apply a little water on one side and stick the wet side around the inside of the pressure cooker till brown spots appear. You can apply 3 to 4 naans at a time inside the walls of the pressure cooker.
3. Remove and apply butter.

⇛ **Serve hot.**

TOASTED ROTI

PICTURE ON PAGE 17

You can serve crisp rotis by toasting them.

PREPARATION TIME: 30 MINUTES. COOKING TIME: 15 MINUTES. MAKES 8 ROTIS.

For the dough

2 teacups wheat flour (gehun ka atta)
5 teaspoons ghee or refined oil
$^1/_2$ teaspoon salt

1. Mix all the ingredients and add enough water to make a semi-stiff dough.
2. Knead well and keep for $^1/_2$ hour. Knead well again and divide into 8 equal portions.
3. Roll out each portion into a thick round with the help of a little flour.

For the stuffing

MINT STUFFING

1 teacup finely chopped mint
2 green chillies, chopped
$^1/_2$ teaspoon salt
$^1/_2$ teaspoon amchur powder
1 tablespoon dried bread crumbs

Mix all the ingredients well.

SPINACH STUFFING

4 teacups finely chopped spinach
2 onions, chopped
2 green chillies, chopped
4 tablespoons crumbled paneer, page 72
2 teaspoons oil
salt to taste

1. Heat the oil and fry the onions for $^1/_2$ minute. Add the green chillies and fry again for a few seconds.
2. Add the spinach and cook for 2 minutes.
3. Drain the water if any.
4. Add the paneer and salt.

CAULIFLOWER AND METHI STUFFING

2 teacups grated cauliflower
1/2 teaspoon cumin seeds
1 onion, chopped
2 green chillies, chopped
1 tablespoon chopped coriander or 2 tablespoons chopped fenugreek (methi) leaves
1/2 teaspoon chopped ginger
2 teaspoons oil
salt to taste

1. Heat the oil and fry the cumin seeds until they crackle.
2. Add the onion, green chillies and ginger and fry again for 1/2 minute.
3. Add the cauliflower and salt, sprinkle a little water and cook until three quarters cooked.
4. Add the coriander and mix well.

ONION STUFFING

1 teacup chopped onion
2 green chillies, chopped
1/2 teaspoon anardana (pomegranate seeds)
2 tablespoons chopped coriander
1/2 teaspoon chilli powder (optional)
salt to taste

1. Sprinkle a little salt over the onion and keep aside for 10 minutes. Squeeze out the water.
2. Roast the anardana lightly on a tava (griddle) and then powder it.
3. Add the onion, coriander, green chillies, chilli powder and salt.

How to proceed

1. Divide the stuffing into 8 equal portions.
2. Brush each dough round with a little oil and spread one stuffing portion on it.
3. Roll out into a cigar shape.
4. Make a small round like a coil and press lightly by hand.
5. Roll out again into a thick roti.
6. Repeat for the remaining dough and stuffing.
7. Cook on a hot tava (griddle) on both sides until pink spots come on top.
8. When you want to serve, put the rotis in a toaster until brown spots appear on each side.

SUBZI PARATHAS

An ideal breakfast dish.

PREPARATION TIME: 15 MINUTES. COOKING TIME: 20 MINUTES. MAKES 12 PARATHAS.

For the dough

1 1/2 teacups plain flour (maida)
1 1/2 teacups wheat flour (gehun ka atta)
1/2 teaspoon salt
1 teaspoon melted butter or ghee
a little milk

For the stuffing

2 teacups finely chopped boiled vegetables (cabbage, cauliflower, green peas, french beans, capsicum)
2 potatoes, boiled and mashed lightly
1 onion, chopped
2 green chillies, chopped
1/2 teaspoon chilli powder
2 pinches garam masala, page 70
2 tablespoons chopped coriander
2 tablespoons ghee
salt to taste

For the dough

1. Mix the plain flour, wheat flour, salt and butter. Add enough milk to make a soft dough.
2. Knead the dough very well and keep aside for 15 minutes.
3. Divide the dough into 12 equal parts and roll out into rounds with the help of a little flour.
4. Cook each round very lightly on a tava and keep in a folded wet napkin.

For the stuffing

1. Heat the ghee, add the onion and cook until soft.
2. Add the vegetables, potatoes, green chillies, chilli powder, garam masala, chopped coriander and salt and cook for 1 or 2 minutes.
3. Remove and cool.

How to proceed

1. Put 2 tablespoons of the stuffing in the centre of each dough round and fold like an envelope from all corners.

2. Put the round on a tava (griddle) with the open edges at the bottom. Cook for a few minutes, turn over on the other side and cook again until crisp.
3. Repeat for the remaining rounds.

⇛ **Serve hot with curds.**

ORIENTAL STYLE STIR-FRIED VEGETABLE PARATHAS

PICTURE ON PAGE 41

A novel type of paratha, stuffed with Chinese stir-fried vegetables.

PREPARATION TIME: 45 MINUTES. COOKING TIME: 20 MINUTES. MAKES 12 PARATHAS.

For the dough

3 teacups plain flour (maida)
1 tablespoon oil
1/2 teaspoon salt

For the stuffing

2 onions, sliced
2 teacups shredded cabbage
1 teacup bean sprouts
1 teacup carrots, coarsely grated
1/2 teaspoon soya sauce
1/2 teaspoon sugar
salt to taste
a pinch Ajinomoto powder (optional)
2 tablespoons oil

For the dough mixture

1. Mix the plain flour, oil and salt. Add a little warm water to make a soft dough.
2. Knead the dough very well for a few minutes. Leave aside for 1/2 hour.

For the stuffing

1. Heat the oil, add the vegetables, Ajinomoto powder and onions and cook for 3 to 4 minutes.
2. Add the soya sauce, sugar and salt. Mix well and cool.

How to proceed

1. Divide the dough into 12 parts and roll out very thinly.
2. Put 2 to 3 tablespoons of the stuffing in the centre of each paratha and lightly fold on all the sides.
3. Put the paratha on a tava (griddle) with the open edges at the bottom. Cook for a few minutes, turn over on the other side and cook again until crisp.
4. Repeat for the remaining parathas and stuffing.

⇛ **Serve hot with chilli garlic sauce.**

DOUBLE DECKER PARATHAS

A new layered paratha with a tasty and colourful carrot and green peas filling.

PREPARATION TIME: 20 MINUTES. COOKING TIME: 30 MINUTES. MAKES 7 PARATHAS.

For the dough

4 teacups wheat flour (gehun ka atta)
2 tablespoons ghee
$^1/_2$ teaspoon salt

For the carrot stuffing

1 teaspoon cumin seeds
3 carrots, grated
2 green chillies, finely chopped
1 teaspoon lemon juice
1 tablespoon ghee
salt to taste

For the green peas stuffing

2 teacups green peas, boiled and mashed
1 teaspoon cumin seeds
2 green chillies, finely chopped
1 tablespoon chopped coriander
1 tablespoon ghee
salt to taste

Other ingredients

ghee for cooking

For the dough

1. Mix the flour, ghee and salt. Add a little warm water to make a soft dough.
2. Knead the dough very well for a few minutes. Leave aside for $1^1/_2$ hours.

For the carrot stuffing

1. Heat the ghee and fry the cumin seeds until they crackle.
2. Add the carrots, chillies, lemon juice and salt and mix well.
3. Cover and cook for 2 minutes.

For the green peas stuffing

1. Heat the ghee and fry the cumin seeds until they crackle.
2. Add the green chillies, coriander and salt and cook for 1 minute.
3. Add the green peas and cook for 1 minute.

How to proceed

1. Divide the dough into 21 balls and roll each ball into thin rounds of equal size.
2. Cook 7 rounds lightly on a tava (griddle).
3. On one uncooked round, spread 1 tablespoon of the carrot stuffing and cover with a cooked round. Then spread 1 tablespoon of the green peas stuffing, put another uncooked round on the top and press firmly to seal the edges.
4. Cook the double decker parathas on a tava (griddle) on both sides with the help of a little ghee.

⇒ **Serve hot.**

Note: You can use any other stuffing combination.

RICE HANDBREAD (APPA)

PREPARATION TIME: 15 MINUTES. COOKING TIME: 20 MINUTES. MAKES 6 APPAS.

2 teacups rice flour
$^{1}/_{4}$ teaspoon salt

1. Put 1 cup of water to boil with the salt.
2. Add the flour and stir till the flour has absorbed the water. Remove from the heat.
3. Knead into a soft dough with a little water as required. Divide the dough into six small balls.
4. On a wooden board, sprinkle a little water. Wet the hand a little and press each ball evenly to a round, lifting it from the board to form an even round.
5. Heat an earthen tava (khapri). Reduce the heat and bake a round on one side. When it leaves the sides, turn it over on the other side. As it rises, press it around the sides till it puffs like a ball.
6. Remove and keep aside in a plate lined with a napkin.
7. Repeat with the remaining rounds.

⇛ **Serve hot.**

RADISH SPINACH PARATHAS

PICTURE ON PAGE 51

Colourful and tasty. Easy to make.

PREPARATION TIME: 25 MINUTES. COOKING TIME: 25 MINUTES. MAKES 12 PARATHAS.

For the dough

1$^{1}/_{2}$ teacups plain flour (maida)
1$^{1}/_{2}$ teacups wheat flour (gehun ka atta)
1 teacup chopped spinach
$^{1}/_{2}$ teaspoon lemon juice
2 tablespoons ghee

Top: Toasted Roti, page 10 & 11;
Bottom : French Beans in Coconut Gravy, page 46. ⇨

1 teaspoon salt

For the stuffing

2 teacups grated radish
2 tablespoons chopped coriander
2 green chillies, chopped
salt to taste

For the dough

1 Blend the spinach and lemon juice with 2 tablespoons of water in a liquidiser.
2. Sieve the flours with the salt. Add the ghee and mix well.
3. Add the spinach mixture. Make a semi-soft dough by adding enough water.

For the stuffing

1. Sprinkle a little salt over the radish. Keep aside for 1/2 hour and squeeze out the water.
2. Add the coriander, green chillies and salt.

How to proceed

1. Roll out thin rotis. Cook them lightly on a tava and keep aside.
2. When you want to serve, take one roti, spread some mixture and turn the other side over it so that it becomes a half moon.
3. Cook on a tava on both sides with a little ghee.

⇛ **Serve hot with fresh curds.**

LAYERED CHAPATIES

An unusual meal by itself.

PREPARATION TIME: 5 MINUTES. COOKING TIME: 30 MINUTES. SERVES 4 TO 6.

For the chapaties

$1^{1}/_{2}$ teacups wheat flour (gehun ka atta)
1 tablespoon ghee or butter
$^{1}/_{2}$ teaspoon salt

⇦ *Top: Subzi ka Salan, page 50;*
Bottom: Hare Mattar ki Puri, page 24.

For dipping the chapaties

- 1/2 teacup milk
- 2 tablespoons plain flour (maida)

For the stuffing

- 2 boiled potatoes
- 2 teacups finely chopped mixed boiled vegetables (french beans, carrots, cauliflower, green peas etc.)
- 1 onion, finely chopped
- 1 tomato, finely chopped
- 1 green chilli, finely chopped
- 1 teaspoon chilli powder
- 1/2 teaspoon turmeric powder
- 1 tablespoon chopped cashewnuts
- 1 tablespoon chopped coriander
- 2 tablespoons ghee
- salt to taste

For the chapaties

1. Mix all the ingredients for the dough together and make a soft dough.
2. Knead very well and leave aside for 1/2 hour.
3. Roll out the dough into thin chapaties about 150 mm. (6") in diameter and cook them lightly on a tava.

For the stuffing

1. Chop the potatoes finely.
2. Heat the ghee, add the onion and cook for 1 minute.
3. Add the tomato and green chilli and fry for 1 minute.
4. Add the potatoes, mixed vegetables, chilli powder, turmeric powder, cashewnuts, coriander and salt.

How to proceed

1. Grease a baking dish. Put a chapati in it and spread a little stuffing.
2. Dip another chapati in the milk and plain flour mixture and place it on the top of the stuffing. Spread a little mixture again and continue ending with a dipped chapati.
3. Pour 2 teaspoons of melted butter on top and bake in a hot oven at 200°C (400°F) for 15 minutes.
4. Cut into slices and serve.

MEXICAN STYLE PARATHAS

A great combination of paneer, cheese and chillies.

PREPARATION TIME: 20 MINUTES. COOKING TIME: 30 MINUTES. MAKES 12 PARATHAS.

For the tortillas

2 teacups plain flour (maida)
1 teacup wheat flour (gehun ka atta)
4 teaspoons oil
$^1/_2$ teaspoon salt

To be mixed into a stuffing

100 grams grated cottage cheese
50 grams grated cooking cheese
1 green chilli, chopped
1 tomato without the pulp
salt to taste

Other ingredients

oil or ghee for cooking

For the tortillas

1. Mix the flours, oil and salt and make a dough by adding enough water.
2. Knead the dough well and keep for 1/2 hour. Knead again.
3. Roll out the dough into 6" to 7" (150 to 170 mm.) diameter thin rounds with the help of a little flour.
4. Cook them lightly on a tava and keep aside.

How to proceed

1. When you want to serve, spread a little stuffing on one tortilla. Put another tortilla on the top and press well so that they stick. Cook on a tava spreading a little oil on both sides. Cook until crisp.
2. Cut into pieces and serve hot.

CORN AND VEGETABLE ROTI

Different types of vegetables in maize flour make the roti healthy and tasty.

PREPARATION TIME: 15 MINUTES. COOKING TIME: 25 MINUTES. MAKES 8 TO 10 ROTIS.

$1^1/_2$ teacups maize flour (makai ka atta)
$^1/_2$ teacup grated cauliflower
$^1/_2$ teacup finely chopped fenugreek (methi) leaves
$^1/_2$ teacup chopped coriander
2 green chillies, chopped
1 potato, boiled
salt to taste

1. Sieve the flour, add the cauliflower, fenugreek, coriander, green chillies and salt.
2. Grate the boiled potato and add to the mixture.
3. Make a soft dough by adding warm water.
4. Divide the dough into 8 to 10 balls. Roll out with the help of a little flour and cook on a tava until soft.

⇛ **Serve hot.**

VARKEY PARATHAS

Rich, traditional parathas.

PREPARATION TIME: 15 MINUTES. COOKING TIME: 20 MINUTES. SERVES 4 TO 6.

2 teacups plain flour (maida)
2 teacups wheat flour (gehun ka atta)
$^1/_4$ teacup rice flour
$^1/_2$ teacup milk
$^1/_2$ teaspoon salt
4 tablespoons ghee

1. Mix the plain flour, wheat flour and salt.
2. Add the milk and enough water to make a soft dough.
3. Mix the rice flour with the ghee and make a smooth paste.

4. Divide the dough into 6 balls. Roll each ball into a chapati of 150 mm. (6") diameter.
5. Spread the rice paste on one side. Put another chapati on the top. Continue in the same way.
6. Roll up like a Swiss roll and cut into rings. Press each ring lightly and roll out again.
7. Cook on a hot tava until golden. Add a little ghee and cook again.

⇛ **Serve hot.**

SPRING ONION PARATHAS WITH CHINESE STUFFING

Non-fried version of onion pancake.

PREPARATION TIME: 10 MINUTES. COOKING TIME: 25 MINUTES. SERVES 4 TO 6.

For the parathas

2 teacups plain flour (maida)
1 teacup wheat flour (gehun ka atta)
4 teaspoons oil
$^1/_2$ teaspoon salt

For the stuffing

2 teacups finely chopped spring onions with leaves
1 tablespoon oil
a pinch Ajinomoto powder
salt to taste

Other ingredients

oil or ghee for cooking

For the parathas

1. Mix the flours, oil and salt and make a dough by adding enough water.
2. Knead the dough well and keep for $^1/_2$ hour. Knead again.
3. Roll out the dough into 150 to 170 mm. (6" to 7") diameter rounds.

For the stuffing

1. Heat the oil and fry the spring onions for 1 minute. Add the

Ajinomoto and salt.
2. Cook for only 1 minute. Cool.

How to proceed

1. Spread the stuffing on one round. Put another round on the top. Spread a little oil on both sides and cook on a tava until crisp.
2. Cut into pieces and serve hot.

HARE MATTAR KI PURI

PICTURE ON PAGE 18

An ideal snack for breakfast.

PREPARATION TIME: 30 MINUTES. COOKING TIME: 20 MINUTES. MAKES 20 PURIS.

For the dough

500 grams plain flour (maida)
2 tablespoons fresh curds
1 level teaspoon baking powder
1 tablespoon ghee or margarine or bütter
1 teaspoon salt

To be mixed into a stuffing

2 teacups boiled green peas
5 finely chopped green chillies
1 teaspoon cumin seeds
1/2 teaspoon lemon juice
1 teaspoon plain flour (maida)
1 teaspoon ghee
salt to taste

Other ingredients

ghee or refined oil for deep frying

For the dough

1. Sieve the flour very well.
2. Add the curds, baking powder, ghee and salt and make a soft dough by adding some more warm water.
3 Knead the dough for at least 6 to 7 minutes.
3. Keep the dough under a wet cloth for at least 1 hour.
5. Knead for 1 minute.
6. Divide the dough into 20 balls and flatten a little.

For the stuffing

1. Mash the green peas and add the green chillies.
2. Heat the ghee, add the cumin seeds and fry until they crackle.
3. Add the mashed green peas, chillies, lemon juice and salt and cook for a few minutes.
4. Sprinkle the flour and cook for 2 to 3 minutes until the mixture becomes dry.

How to proceed

1. Roll out each ball of dough into a small round. Put a teaspoon of the stuffing in the centre and close it.
2. Roll out thinly with the help of a little flour.
3. Deep fry in ghee.

⇛ **Serve hot.**

STUFFED SHAHI PURIS

Methi puri with paneer stuffing.

PREPARATION TIME: 15 MINUTES. COOKING TIME: 20 MINUTES. MAKES 12 PURIS.

For the dough

2 teacups fenugreek (methi) leaves, finely chopped
2 teacups wheat flour or plain flour (maida)
$^1/_4$ teaspoon baking powder
1 tablespoon fresh curds
2 tablespoons melted ghee

To be mixed into a stuffing

100 grams grated paneer, page 72
3 to 4 chopped green chillies
2 tablespoons chopped coriander
salt to taste

Other ingredients

ghee for deep frying

For the dough mixture

1. Sprinkle salt over the chopped fenugreek leaves and leave aside. After 15 minutes, squeeze out the water.
2. Mix the fenugreek and the flour, baking powder, curds and melted ghee and make a dough by adding a little water.

3. Divide the dough into 12 balls and roll out each ball into a small round.

How to proceed
1. Put 1 teaspoon of the stuffing in one round, fold the edges towards the centre and close. Roll out again.
2. Repeat for the remaining rounds and stuffing.
3. Deep fry in ghee.

⇛ **Serve hot.**

ALOO KI PURI

Fluffy and rich.

PREPARATION TIME: 15 MINUTES. COOKING TIME: 20 MINUTES. SERVES 4 TO 6.

3 teacups plain flour (maida)
2 boiled potatoes
2 pinches pepper powder
$^1/_2$ teacup milk
2 pinches saffron
2 tablespoons melted ghee
$^1/_2$ teaspoon salt
ghee for deep frying

1. Peel and grate the potatoes. Make a smooth paste.
2. Add the flour, pepper, ghee and salt and mix well.
3. Mix the saffron in the milk and add to the flour. If you like, add a little saffron colour to the milk.
4. Knead the dough very well. Keep aside for 1 hour.
5. Roll into small puris and deep fry in hot ghee until they puff up.

⇛ **Serve hot.**

Variation: SPICY ALOO PURI
2 tablespoons chopped coriander
2 green chillies, chopped
$^1/_2$ teaspoon lightly crushed cumin seeds

Add the above ingredients at step 2 and follow the same method.

BHATURAS

Serve them with chole.

PREPARATION TIME: 30 MINUTES. COOKING TIME: 15 MINUTES. MAKES 20 BHATURAS.

500 grams plain flour (maida)
$1^1/_2$ teaspoons sugar
20 grams fresh yeast or 2 teaspoons dry yeast
2 tablespoons fresh curds
25 grams ghee or margarine or butter
1 teaspoon salt

Other ingredients

oil for deep frying

1. Sieve the flour very well.
2. Mix the sugar and yeast in 1 teacup of warm water and stir until the yeast dissolves. Cover and wait for 5 to 7 minutes until the mixture is full of froth.
3. Add this liquid along with the curds, ghee and salt to the flour and make a soft dough by adding some more warm water.
4. Knead the dough for at least 6 to 7 minutes.
5. Keep the dough under a wet cloth for 30 minutes.
6. Knead for 1 minute.
7. Divide the dough into 20 small pieces and roll out puris with the help of a little flour.
8. Deep fry the puris in oil.

⇛ **Serve hot.**

BANANA DOSA

PICTURE ON PAGE 36

A novel way of presenting a dosa. Spongy and soft.

PREPARATION TIME: 20 MINUTES. COOKING TIME: 30 MINUTES. MAKES 30 TO 40 DOSAS.

2 teacups rice
$^1/_2$ teacup urad dal
2 pinches fenugreek (methi) seeds
3 bananas
2 green chillies, chopped
1 teaspoon sugar
salt to taste
ghee or butter for frying

1. Soak the rice, dal and fenugreek seeds for at least 5 to 6 hours.
2. Drain and grind to a fine paste.
3. Add a little warm water and salt. The dosa mixture should be like a thick white sauce. Keep aside for 5 to 6 hours.
4. Mash the bananas. Add to the dosa mixture. Add the green chillies and sugar.
5. Grease a a non-stick frying pan with a little oil and heat.
6. Spread the mixture in small rounds about 50 mm. (2") diameter. Put a little ghee around the sides of the rounds and cook for a few minutes.
7. Turn and cook again.

⇒ **Serve hot with chutney.**

SUBZIS

SUBZI KA KORMA

A delicately flavoured, moderately spiced dry vegetable.

PREPARATION TIME: 15 MINUTES. COOKING TIME: 5 MINUTES. SERVES 6.

4 teacups mixed boiled vegetables (french beans, carrots, green peas, cauliflower), cut into big cubes
1 onion, chopped
2 potatoes, boiled and cubed
2 tablespoons chopped coriander
$^1/_2$ teaspoon garam masala, page 70
1 teaspoon lemon juice
2 tablespoons ghee or refined oil
salt to taste

To be ground into a paste

6 to 7 green chillies
25 mm. (1") piece ginger
1 onion

1. Heat the ghee and fry the onion for 1 minute.
2. Add the paste and fry again for 1 minute.
3. Add the vegetables, potatoes, coriander, garam masala, lemon juice and salt and cook for a few minutes, stirring occasionally.

⇛ **Serve hot.**

SHAHI ALOO

PICTURE ON PAGE 35

You will love this easy-to-make vegetable.

PREPARATION TIME : 15 MINUTES. COOKING TIME: 15 MINUTES. SERVES 4.

12 small round potatoes
1 large tomato, chopped
2 tablespoons fresh curds
1 teaspoon chilli powder
6 cashewnuts

1 tablespoon raisins
$^1/_2$ teaspoon sugar
3 tablespoons oil
salt to taste
oil for deep frying

To be ground into a paste

1 stick cinnamon
seeds of 2 cardamoms
3 cloves
6 black peppercorns
1 teaspoon coriander seeds
$^1/_2$ teaspooon cumin seeds
1 teaspoon poppy seeds (khus khus)
12 mm. ($^1/_2$") piece ginger
3 cloves garlic
$^1/_2$ teaspoon chilli powder

For the topping

2 tablespoons chopped coriander

1. Prick the potatoes with a fork and deep fry them in oil until soft. Remove and keep aside.
2. Heat 3 tablespoons of oil and fry the paste for 1 to 2 minutes.
3. Add the tomato, curds and chilli powder and fry for 1 minute. Add the cashewnuts and raisins and fry for 1 minute more.
4. Add the potatoes with $^1/_2$ teacup of water and cook for 3 to 4 minutes.
5. Add the sugar and salt.

⇛ **Sprinkle coriander on top and serve hot with puris or parathas.**

SHAHI GOBHI

This popular Moghlai vegetable is lightly spiced.

PREPARATION TIME : 15 MINUTES. COOKING TIME : 20 MINUTES. SERVES 6.

1 large cauliflower, divided into florets
1 onion, sliced
2 cardamoms
2 cloves

2 bay leaves
1/2 teaspoon sugar
1 large tomato
1 teacup beaten curds
1 teacup boiled green peas
2 tablespoons fresh cream
3 tablespoons ghee or refined oil
salt to taste

To be ground into a paste

2 cardamoms
3 cloves
2 teaspoons coriander seeds
1/2 teaspoon cumin seeds
1 bay leaf
4 cloves garlic
25 mm. (1") piece ginger
1 stick cinnamon
1/2 teaspoon turmeric powder
1 medium onion
1 tablespoon chopped cashewnuts
1 teaspoon chilli powder

For the topping

3 tablespoons chopped coriander

1. Parboil the cauliflower for 6 minutes. Drain and set aside.
2. Put the tomato in hot water for 10 minutes. Remove and blend into a purée.
3. Heat the ghee and fry the onion until golden. Add the cardamoms, cloves, bay leaves and sugar and fry for 2 to 3 minutes.
4. Add the paste and fry for 3 to 4 minutes or until the ghee rises to the top.
5. Add the tomato purée and curds and fry for 2 to 3 minutes. Add the peas, cauliflower and salt and simmer for 2 to 3 minutes.
6. Add the cream and garnish with the coriander.

⇛ **Serve hot.**

KADAI PANEER

The all-time favourite vegetable.

PREPARATION TIME: 20 MINUTES. COOKING TIME: 10 MINUTES. SERVES 6.

250 grams paneer, page 72
3 onions, finely chopped
2 teaspoons coriander-cumin seed powder
$^1/_4$ teaspoon turmeric powder
1 teaspoon chilli powder
1 teaspoon garam masala, page 70
1 teaspoon kasuri methi (dried fenugreek leaves)
5 medium tomatoes
1 capsicum, sliced
100 grams fresh cream
a pinch sugar
3 tablespoons ghee or refined oil
salt to taste
ghee or refined oil for deep frying

To be ground into a paste

4 cloves garlic
12 mm. ($^1/_2$") piece ginger

1. Cut the paneer into wide strips and deep fry lightly in ghee. Place in lukewarm water.
2. Put the tomatoes in hot water for 10 minutes. Remove and blend into a purée.
3. Heat 3 tablespoons of ghee and fry the onions until golden. Add the paste and fry for 1/2 minute.
4. Add the coriander-cumin seed powder, turmeric and chilli powders, garam masala and kasuri methi and fry again for 1 minute.
5. Add the tomato purée and capsicum, cover and cook for 4 to 5 minutes.
6. Add the paneer and salt and cook for 2 to 3 minutes.
7. Finally, add the cream and sugar and serve hot.

SPICY CORN

Peanuts add a new flavour to the gravy.

PREPARATION TIME : 20 MINUTES. COOKING TIME : 30 MINUTES. SERVES 6.

6 tender fresh corn cobs
1 onion, chopped
1 teaspoon chopped green chilli
1 teaspoon chopped ginger
3 tomatoes
3 tablespoons peanuts
2 tablespoons oil
salt to taste

1. Cut the corn into 37 mm. ($1^1/_2$") round pieces. Boil the corn in salted water in a pressure cooker until tender.
2. Roast the peanuts on a tava. Take out the skin and pound them.
3. Heat the oil and fry the onion until golden.
4. Add the green chilli and ginger and cook for a few seconds.
5. Add the tomatoes and cook until they are soft.
6. Add the peanuts and $^1/_2$ cup of water and cook for a while.
7. Add the corn and salt.

⇛ **Serve hot.**

HARI BHAJI

Vegetables made with fresh herbs.

PREPARATION TIME : 10 MINUTES. COOKING TIME : 12 MINUTES. SERVES 6.

$1^1/_2$ teacups finely chopped spinach
1 tablespoon chopped dill (suva bhaji)
1 tablespoon chopped mint (phudina)
a few drops lemon juice
a pinch soda bicarb
1 capsicum, chopped
2 teacups mixed boiled vegetables (french beans, carrots, green peas, cauliflower), cut into cubes
1 onion, chopped
1 tomato, chopped
1 tablespoon butter

1 tablespoon kasuri methi (dried fenugreek leaves)
1 teaspoon coriander-cumin seed powder
$^{1}/_{2}$ teaspoon garam masala, page 70
2 tablespoons oil
salt to taste

To be ground into paste no.1

4 cloves garlic
12 mm. ($^{1}/_{2}$") piece ginger
3 green chillies

To be ground into paste no.2

1 tablespoon cashewnuts
1 tablespoon poppy seeds (khus khus)

For the topping

2 tablespoons chopped coriander

1. Cook the spinach, dill, mint, lemon juice and soda bicarb with $^{1}/_{2}$ teacup of water.
2. When cooked, blend in a liquidiser.
3. Heat the oil and fry the onion until golden. Then add the paste no.1 and fry for a few seconds. Add the kasurı methi, coriander-cumin seeds powder and garam masala and fry for a few seconds.
4. Then add the vegetables, capsicum, tomato, a little water and salt and cook for a few minutes. Add the spinach mixture, paste no.2 and the butter and cook for a few minutes.

⇛ **Serve hot topped with coriander leaves.**

METHI MUTTER MALAI

PICTURE ON PAGE 42

A tasty combination of fenugreek and green peas.

PREPARATION TIME: 20 MINUTES. COOKING TIME: 15 MINUTES. SERVES 6.

3 teacups chopped fenugreek (methi) leaves
$^{1}/_{2}$ teaspoon cumin seeds
1 onion, chopped
2 large tomatoes

Top: Masala Paneer Naan, page 8; Bottom: Shahi Aloo, page 29. ⇨

1 teacup boiled green peas
1 teacup milk
a pinch sugar
3 tablespoons oil
salt to taste

To be ground into a paste

1 onion
4 green chillies
25 mm. (1") piece ginger
3 cloves garlic
2 tablespoons cashewnuts
2 teaspoons khus khus (poppy seeds)

For the dry masala (to be roasted lightly and powdered)

2 small sticks cinnamon
4 cloves
2 cardamoms
4 peppercorns
1 teaspoon cumin seeds

1. Wash the fenugreek leaves. Add $^{1}/_{2}$ teaspoon of salt. Wait for 15 minutes and then squeeze out the water.
2. Put the tomato in hot water for 10 minutes. Remove and blend into a purée.
3. Heat 2 tablespoons of oil, add the cumin seeds and fry until they crackle. Add the fenugreek and cook for 3 to 4 minutes. Remove the fenugreek.
4. Add the balance 1 tablespoon of oil and heat again. Add the onion and fry until golden.
5. Add the paste and fry for 1 minute. Add the tomato purée and the dry masala and fry again. Add the peas, fenugreek, milk, sugar, salt and a little water and cook for a few minutes.

⇛ **Serve hot**

⇦ *Clockwise from Top: Bhindi Dahi (Kerala Style), page 67; Banana Dosa, page 28 ; Moongfali (Groundnut) Potato Vegetable, page 64.*

PANEER MAKHANWALA

Tasty but not spicy. Cooked in cream and tomato sauce.

PREPARATION TIME : 25 MINUTES. COOKING TIME : 30 MINUTES. SERVES 8.

300 grams paneer, page 72
3 onions, sliced
1 teacup fresh cream
2 level tablespoons plain flour (maida)
1 teacup milk
4 tablespoons tomato ketchup
2 tablespoons butter
1/2 teaspoon chilli powder
ghee for deep frying
salt to taste

1. Cut the paneer into long strips.
2. Deep fry the paneer strips lightly in ghee. Place the paneer in water.
3. Mix the cream, flour, milk and tomato ketchup.
5. Heat the butter and fry the onions until pale in colour.
6. Add the paneer, cream mixture, chilli powder and salt and cook on a very slow flame for 10 minutes.

⇛ **Serve hot with parathas.**

PANEER IN QUICK WHITE GRAVY

A mildly flavoured vegetable made with very soft paneer.

PREPARATION TIME : 10 MINUTES. COOKING TIME : 10 MINUTES. SERVES 4.

250 grams fresh paneer, page 72
3 tablespoons fresh cream
1/4 teaspoon garam masala, page 70
2 tablespoons milk
2 tablespoons ghee

To be ground into a paste

1 large onion

1 tablespoon cashewnut
4 cloves garlic
6 mm. ($^1/_4$") piece ginger

1. Cut the paneer in very small cubes. If it is not soft, keep it in warm water for at least 2 hours.
2. Heat the ghee and fry the paste. Add the garam masala and fry again.
3. Add the paneer, cream, milk and 2 tablespoons of water and cook for a few minutes.

⇛ **Serve hot.**

PANEER TIKKI PASANDA

Paneer tikkis served in a gravy rich in herbs and spices.

PREPARATION TIME: 25 MINUTES. COOKING TIME: 10 MINUTES. SERVES 4 TO 6.

For the tikkis

300 grams paneer, page 72
2 green chillies, chopped
$^1/_4$ teaspoon pepper powder
2 tablespoons plain flour (maida)
bread crumbs
oil for cooking
salt to taste

For the paste no.1

2 onions, roughly chopped
5 cloves garlic
12 mm. ($^1/_2$") piece ginger
2 tablespoons cashewnuts

For the paste no.2

2 onions, sliced

Other ingredients

2 tablespoons oil or ghee
1 teacup beaten curds
$^1/_2$ teaspoon garam masala, page 70
1 teaspoon chilli powder
salt to taste

For the tikkis

1. Mash the paneer well.
2. Add the green chillies, pepper powder, flour and salt and mix well.
3. Shape into tikkis and roll in bread crumbs.
4. Cook on a non-stick tava by applying oil while cooking.

For the paste no.1

1. Boil the onions in 1 cup of water until soft.
2. Add the garlic, ginger and cashewnuts and make a paste.

For the paste no.2

Deep fry the onions in ghee or oil until golden and make a paste by putting in a grinder.

How to proceed

1. Heat the oil in a vessel. Add the paste no.1 and cook on a low flame for a few minutes.
2. Add the chilli powder and garam masala, mix and cook again.
3. Take the vessel off the fire and add the beaten curds. Mix well and go on stirring all the time.
4. Cook for a while. Add the paste no.2 and salt.
5. Arrange the paneer tikkis in a plate. Pour the boiling gravy on the top.

⇛ **Serve hot.**

FRESH MUSHROOM CURRY

Using fresh coriander and boiled onion paste enhances the taste of the gravy and makes it a delicacy.

PREPARATION TIME: 10 MINUTES. COOKING TIME: 10 MINUTES. SERVES 4 TO 6.

250 grams fresh mushrooms
2 cardamoms
2 bay leaves
3 cloves
$^{1}/_{2}$ teaspoon garam masala, page 70
$^{1}/_{2}$ teaspoon chilli powder

Top: Oriental Style Stir-fried Vegetable Parathas, page 13; Bottom: Malai Kofta Curry, page 46. ⇨

1 teaspoon finely chopped ginger
2 green chillies, chopped
1 teacup beaten curds
$^1/_2$ teacup chopped coriander
4 tablespoons ghee or refined oil
salt to taste

For the paste

2 onions
6 cloves garlic
12 mm. ($^1/_2$") piece ginger
3 tablespoons cashewnuts

For the paste

1. Boil the onions in 1 cup of water until soft.
2. Add the garlic, ginger and cashewnuts and make a paste.

How to proceed

1. Slice the mushrooms and put them in hot water for 2 minutes. Drain.
2. Heat the ghee and add the cardamoms, bay leaves and cloves and fry for a few seconds.
3. Add the paste and fry again for 2 to 3 minutes. Add the garam masala, chilli powder, ginger and green chillies and fry again for $^1/_2$ minute.
4. Take the vessel off the fire and add the curds. Mix well.
5. Put the vessel on a slow flame and go on stirring all the time.
6. Add the mushrooms, coriander and salt and cook for a few minutes.

⇛ **Serve hot.**

⇦ *Clockwise from Top: Methi Mattar Malai, page 34; Paneer in Coconut Gravy, page 44; Quick Baby Corn & Paneer Subzi, page 61.*

PANEER IN COCONUT GRAVY

PICTURE ON PAGE 42

This unusually cooked paneer vegetable tastes great.

PREPARATION TIME : 20 MINUTES. COOKING TIME : 30 MINUTES. SERVES 4.

250 grams paneer, page 72
1 coconut
1 tablespoon cornflour
1 teaspoon cumin seeds
1 tablespoon oil
ghee or refined oil for deep frying
salt to taste

To be ground into a paste

3 green chillies
1 medium onion
25 mm. (1") piece ginger

For the topping

1 tablespoon chopped coriander

1. Cut the paneer into cubes or slices and deep fry in ghee to a light pink colour. Place in lukewarm water.
2. Scrape out the coconut meat, add $1^1/_2$ teacups of water and blend in a blender. Strain and take out thick milk. Add the cornflour and mix well.
3. Heat the oil and fry the cumin seeds until they crackle. Add the paste and fry for 2 minutes.
4. Add the coconut milk and cook for 10 minutes. Remove from the heat and add the paneer slices and salt.
5. Cook for a few minutes.

⇛ **Serve hot sprinkled with coriander.**

PHOOLGOBHI AUR MUTTER KI KARI (CAULIFLOWER AND PEAS CURRY)

A coconut-based curry gives this vegetable a delicious flavour.

PREPARATION TIME : 15 MINUTES. COOKING TIME : 20 MINUTES. SERVES 6.

2 teacups cauliflower, divided into small florets
1 teacup green peas, boiled
2 bay leaves
2 tomatoes
2 teaspoons fresh curds
2 tablespoons chopped cashewnuts
$^1/_2$ teaspoon sugar
3 tablespoons ghee or refined oil
salt to taste

To be ground into a paste

1 onion, chopped
2 tablespoons grated coconut
5 garlic cloves
2 coriander seeds
1 teaspoon cumin seeds
12 mm. ($^1/_2$") piece ginger
2 teaspoons poppy seeds (khus khus)
6 red chillies

1. Put the tomatoes in hot water for 10 minutes. Remove and blend into a purée.
2. Heat the ghee, add the cauliflower florets and gently fry for 6 to 7 minutes. Remove and keep aside.
3. In the same ghee, add the bay leaves and paste and fry for 2 to 3 minutes. Add the tomato purée and curds and fry for 2 to 3 minutes.
4. Add the cauliflower, green peas, cashewnuts, sugar, $^1/_2$ cup of water and salt and cook for 5 to 7 minutes until the vegetables are soft.

⇛ **Serve hot.**

FRENCH BEANS IN COCONUT GRAVY

PICTURE ON PAGE 17

The crunchiness of peanuts along with coconut milk makes this a tasty vegetable.

PREPARATION TIME: 15 MINUTES. COOKING TIME : 20 MINUTES. SERVES 6.

400 grams french beans
a pinch asafoetida
a pinch soda bicarb
1 coconut
3 to 4 green chillies, coarsely chopped
2 tablespoons lightly roasted peanuts
2 tablespoons oil
salt to taste

1. Scrape out the coconut meat, add the green chillies and 2 cups of water. Blend in a blender and strain.
2. String the french beans and slice them diagonally.
3. Heat the oil, add the asafoetida and the french beans.
4. Add $^3/_4$ cup of water and the soda bicarb. Cook on a slow flame until the french beans are soft.
5. Add the roasted peanuts, coconut milk and salt to the cooked french beans and cook for a few minutes.

⇛ **Serve hot.**

MALAI KOFTA CURRY

PICTURE ON PAGE 41

A tasty kofta curry.

PREPARATION TIME : 30 MINUTES. COOKING TIME : 40 MINUTES. SERVES 6.

For the koftas
100 grams green peas
100 grams cauliflower, finely chopped

100 grams french beans, finely chopped
100 grams carrots, finely chopped
250 grams potatoes, boiled and mashed
2 tablespoons bread crumbs
1 bread slice, soaked in water
1 teaspoon garam masala, page 70
1 teaspoon chilli powder
1½ teaspoons lemon juice
salt to taste
oil for deep frying

To be ground into a paste (for the koftas)

9 cloves garlic
25 mm. (1") piece ginger
7 green chillies

For the gravy

750 grams tomatoes
3 onions
4 cloves
2 small sticks cinnamon
1 tablespoon cornflour
1 teaspoon sugar
1 teaspoon garam masala, page 70
1 teaspoon chilli powder
4 tablespoons butter
salt and pepper to taste

To be ground into a paste (for the gravy)

15 cloves garlic
25 mm. (1") piece ginger
5 green chillies

For baking

1 tablespoon fresh cream
½ tablespoon grated cheese

For the koftas

1. Boil the peas.
2. Steam the cauliflower, french beans and carrots in a pressure cooker without adding water.
3. Add the vegetables and peas to the potatoes and make a dough.
4. Add 1 tablespoon of bread crumbs and the bread slice.

5. Add the paste, garam masala, chilli powder, lemon juice and salt and form into kofta balls.
6. Roll the koftas into the remaining bread crumbs and deep fry in oil to a golden brown colour. Keep aside.

For the gravy

1. Put the tomatoes in hot water for 10 minutes. Remove and blend into a purée.
2. Blend the onions in a liquidiser with very little water.
3. Heat the butter, add the onions and stir fry for 5 minutes till light brown.
4. Then add the cloves, cinnamon and paste and fry again for 2 minutes.
5. Add the tomato purée and cook for 2 minutes.
6. Add 1 teacup of water and boil for 3 to 4 minutes.
7. Pour the mixture into a blender, add the cornflour and sugar and blend.
8. Put to cook again and add the garam masala, chilli powder, salt and pepper and cook for 5 minutes.

How to proceed

1. Arrange the koftas in an ovenproof dish. Pour the gravy and fresh cream over the koftas.
2. Sprinkle the grated cheese on top and bake or grill for 10 to 15 minutes in a hot oven at 200°C (400°F) until the cheese melts.

SPINACH KOFTAS

Tasty koftas with a rich gravy.

PREPARATION TIME: 20 MINUTES. COOKING TIME: 30 MINUTES. SERVES 6.

For the koftas

3 teacups chopped spinach
4 tablespoons gram flour (besan)
2 slices fresh bread, crumbled
1/2 teaspoon ground ginger
salt to taste

For the stuffing (for the koftas)

4 to 5 tablespoons paneer, page 72
1 tablespoon chopped coriander

1 green chilli, chopped
8 to 10 raisins

Other ingredients (for the koftas)

oil for deep frying

For the gravy

4 large tomatoes
1 teaspoon chilli powder
100 grams fresh cream
4 tablespoons ghee
salt to taste

To be ground into a paste (for the gravy)

1 large onion
2 tablespoons grated fresh coconut
7 cloves garlic
2 green chillies
2 red chillies
2 teaspoons coriander seeds
1 teaspoon cumin seeds
2 tablespoons cherongia sapick (charoli)
2 teaspoons poppy seeds (khus khus)
25 mm. (1") piece ginger
2 tablespoons chopped coriander

For the gravy

1. Cut the tomatoes into big pieces, add 4 cups of water and cook. When soft, prepare a soup by passing through a sieve.
2. Heat the ghee in a vessel and fry the paste very well.
3. Add the chilli powder and fry again for 1 minute.
4. Add the tomato soup, cream and salt and boil the gravy for at least 10 to 15 minutes.

For the koftas

1. Steam the spinach leaves for 5 minutes, then squeeze out the water.
2. Roast the gram flour on a tava for 2 to 3 minutes.
3. Mix the spinach, roasted gram flour, bread, ginger and salt very well.
4. Mix all the ingredients together for the stuffing.
5. Make small balls of the spinach mixture and flatten them

slightly. Put a little mixture of the stuffing in the centre and close it. Repeat for the remaining spinach mixture and stuffing.

6. Deep fry the koftas in oil. Remove, drain and keep aside.

How to serve

Just before serving, add the koftas to the hot gravy.

⇛ **Serve hot.**

SUBZI KA SALAN (VEGETABLE CURRY)

PICTURE ON PAGE 18

A light vegetable with a nice aroma.

PREPARATION TIME: 15 MINUTES. COOKING TIME: 20 MINUTES. SERVES 6.

2 tomatoes
3 teacups mixed boiled vegetables (french beans, carrots, green peas, cauliflower, potatoes), cut into big pieces
1 coconut
1 onion, chopped
3 green chillies, finely chopped
1 teaspoon chilli powder
$^1/_2$ teaspoon turmeric powder
1 teacup fresh curds
3 tablespoons ghee or oil
salt to taste

To be ground to a dry powder

3 cloves
3 black peppercorns
3 cardamoms
$^1/_2$ teaspoon grated nutmeg

1. Scrape out the coconut meat, add 3 cups of water and blend in a blender. Strain the coconut milk.

Clockwise from Top: Hare Chana ki Kari with Methi Muthia, page 53; Radish Spinach Parathas, page 16; Kand, Paneer and Peas Chaat, page 66; ⇨

2. Put the tomatoes in hot water for 10 minutes. Remove and blend into a purée.
3. Heat the ghee, add the onion and fry until golden. Add the green chillies.
4. Mix the chilli powder and turmeric powder with a little water. Add to the onion and fry for a few seconds.
5. Add the tomato purée and curds and fry for a few minutes. Add the vegetables and fry again.
6. Add the coconut milk and bring to a boil.
7. Sprinkle the dry powder over the vegetables and cook for a few minutes. Add salt.

⇛ **Serve hot.**

HARE CHANA KI KARI WITH METHI MUTHIA

PICTURE ON PAGE 51

When fresh chanas are not available in season, you can use dry chanas. Soak and boil before using.

PREPARATION TIME : 15 MINUTES. COOKING TIME : 15 MINUTES. SERVES 6.

2 teacups moong sprouts or
2 teacups fresh chana
1 coconut
1 onion, chopped
1 teaspoon cornflour
oil
salt to taste

To be ground into a paste
1 teacup chopped coriander
7 green chillies
12 mm. ($^1/_2$") piece ginger
6 cloves garlic
2 teaspoons lemon juice
4 to 5 spinach leaves

⇦ *Clockwise from Top: Stuffed Vegetables, page 62; Dhokla Corn Subzi, page 63.*

For the methi muthias

2 teacups chopped methi bhaji
1/2 teacup wheat flour (gehun ka atta)
a pinch asafoetida
1 teaspoon sugar
1 teaspoon chilli powder or
1 teaspoon green chilli-ginger paste
2 tablespoons hot oil
oil for deep frying

For the garnish

chopped coriander

1. Boil the chana (or the moong sprouts). For boiling the chana, add a pinch of soda bi-carb.
2. Scrape out the coconut meat, add 2 cups of water and blend in a blender. Strain the coconut milk.
3. Heat the oil and fry the onion for 1 minute. Add the paste and fry for 3 to 4 minutes.
4. Add the chana or the sprouts.
5. Mix the cornflour in the coconut milk, add salt and add to the chana mixture.
6. Mix all the ingredients for the methi muthias including the hot oil. Shape into small balls and deep fry in oil on a slow flame.
7. Add these balls to the curry.

⇛ **Serve hot decorated with fresh coriander.**

MIXED VEGETABLE KOFTA CURRY

A rich white gravy enriched with gram flour.

PREPARATION TIME : 20 MINUTES. COOKING TIME : 25 MINUTES. SERVES 6.

For the koftas

4 tablespoons finely chopped aubergine
1 onion, chopped
1/2 teacup grated cabbage
2 green chillies, finely chopped

4 tablespoons gram flour (besan)
2 pinches soda bi-carb
salt
oil for deep frying

To be ground into a paste

2 tablespoons khus khus
2 tablespoons broken cashewnuts
6 to 8 garlic cloves
25 mm. (1") piece ginger
4 green chillies
2 large tomatoes
1 tablespoon grated coconut

To be ground into a dry masala

2 small sticks cinnamon
3 cloves
2 cardamoms

Other ingredients

2 tablespoons ghee
2 tablespoons gram flour (besan)
1/2 teaspoon chilli powder
1/2 teacup tamarind water, page 72
salt to taste
2 tablespoons fresh cream

For the koftas

1. Mix all the ingredients for the koftas (except the oil) with a little water and make a batter.
2. Heat the oil and when hot, drop teaspoonfuls of the batter and cook for about 3 minutes until golden brown.
3. Remove with a slotted spoon.
4. Repeat with the remaining batter.

How to proceed

1. Heat the ghee and fry the paste for 2 minutes.
2. Add the gram flour and chilli powder and fry again for 1 minute. Then add the tamarind water, dry masala mixture and salt and boil for 5 minutes.
3. Just before serving, add the koftas and the cream and bring to a boil.

⇒ **Serve hot.**

BAKED METHI CHAMAN

A popular methi paneer with a Western touch.

PREPARATION TIME : 15 MINUTES. COOKING TIME : 30 MINUTES. SERVES 6.

4 teacups chopped spinach
1 teacup chopped fenugreek (methi) leaves
a pinch soda bicarb
1 onion, chopped
1 green chilli, chopped
100 grams fresh paneer, page 72, cut into small pieces
2 tablespoons ghee or refined oil
salt to taste

For the potato layer

3 potatoes, boiled and mashed coarsely
2 tablespoons chopped coriander
1 teaspoon chopped green chillies
1 teaspoon lemon juice
salt to taste

For the covering

100 grams beaten cream or 1 teacup white sauce
4 tablespoons grated cheese

For the potato layer

Mix together all the ingredients.

How to proceed

1. Boil the spinach and the fenugreek leaves in 2 tablespoons of water with a pinch of soda bicarb until soft. Drain and blend in a blender.
2. Heat the ghee and fry the onion until golden in colour. Add the green chilli and fry again for a few seconds. Add the spinach and fenugreek.
3. Add the paneer pieces and salt. If required, add a little lemon juice.
4. Spread the potato layer evenly at the bottom of a baking dish and spread the spinach mixture on the top.
5. Cover with the beaten cream and cheese and bake in a hot oven at 200°C (400°F) for 15 to 20 minutes.

⇒ **Serve hot.**

ORIENTAL CURRY

A popular version of coconut curry from Thailand.

PREPARATION TIME : 10 MINUTES. COOKING TIME : 10 MINUTES. SERVES 6.

3 teacups mixed boiled vegetables (carrots, french beans, cauliflower, green peas, potatoes), cut into big pieces
1 coconut
3 tablespoons oil
salt to taste

To be ground into a paste
1 onion
5 tablespoons chopped coriander
4 green chillies
12 mm. (1/2") piece ginger
1/2 teaspoon lemon juice
4 cloves garlic

To be ground to a dry powder
3 cloves
3 black peppercorns
3 cardamoms
2 teaspoons grated nutmeg

1. Scrape out the coconut meat, add 3 cups of water and blend in a blender. Strain the coconut milk.
2. Dry roast the powder.
3. Heat the oil, add the paste and fry for 3 to 4 minutes.
4. Add the vegetables, coconut milk and salt and cook for a few minutes.
5. Add the dry powder and cook for a while.

⇛ **Serve hot.**

BAKED CABBAGE

An attractive dish.

PREPARATION TIME : 20 MINUTES. COOKING TIME : 30 MINUTES. SERVES 6.

1 medium cabbage
1 teacup boiled green peas
2 tablespoons fresh cream
2 tablespoons grated cheese

To be ground into a paste (for the gravy)

1 onion, chopped
2 tomatoes, chopped
4 red dry chillies
2 small sticks cinnamon
3 cloves
12 mm. ($^{1}/_{2}$") piece ginger
4 cloves garlic

For the gravy

2 tablespoons butter
1 onion, chopped
1 bay leaf
$^{1}/_{2}$ teaspoon sugar
salt to taste

For the gravy

1. Melt the butter over low heat. Add the onion and bay leaf and cook for 1 minute.
2. Add the paste and cook for 3 to 4 minutes. Add 1 cup of water, the sugar and salt and boil for a few minutes.

How to proceed

1. Put the cabbage into a vessel of boiling water and cook for a few minutes until cooked. Remove from the water and keep aside.
2. Put the cabbage in a serving dish. Cut out and remove any hard stem in the center with a sharp knife.
3. Pour over the gravy. Sprinkle the peas on top. Spread a little cream and top with the cheese.
4. Bake in a hot oven at 200°C (400°F) for 10 to 15 minutes until golden brown.

⇛ **Serve hot.**

SHAHI BAKED PANEER

A popular Moghlai dish.

PREPARATION TIME : 20 MINUTES. COOKING TIME : 40 MINUTES. SERVES 6.

450 grams paneer, page 72
100 grams green peas, boiled
2 tomatoes
3 onions, grated
2 sticks cinnamon
2 bay leaves
2 cloves
1 teaspoon chilli powder
200 grams fresh curds
$1^1/_2$ teaspoons garam masala, page 70
2 teaspoons freshly ground roasted cumin seeds
1 teaspoon coriander powder
2 tablespoons fresh cream
2 tablespoons ghee
sugar and salt to taste
ghee or refined oil for deep frying

For the paste

1 tablespoon poppy seeds (khus-khus)
1 tablespoon chopped cashewnuts
2 tablespoons milk
25 mm. (1") piece ginger
5 cloves garlic

For baking

1 tablespoon grated cheese
1 tablespoon fresh cream

For the paste

Put the poppy seeds and cashewnuts in the milk and allow to soak for 30 minutes. Then, grind to a paste with the ginger and garlic.

For the paneer

1. Cut three quarters of the paneer into small cubes. Crumble the remaining paneer.
2. Deep fry the paneer cubes in ghee or oil until golden.
3. Put the tomatoes in hot water for 10 minutes. Remove and blend into a purée.

4. Heat the ghee and fry the onions until light pink.
5. Add the cinnamon, bay leaves and cloves and fry for 2 minutes. Add the chilli powder and $1^1/_2$ cups of water and cook for 1 minute.
6. Add the tomato purée and bring to the boil.
7. Add the curds, garam masala, cumin seed powder, coriander powder and the paste.
8. Add the green peas and fried paneer and cook for 5 minutes.
9. Finally, add the crumbled paneer, fresh cream, sugar and salt and cook for 1 minute.

How to proceed

1. Sprinkle the grated cheese on top.
2. Dot with the cream and bake in a hot oven at 230°C (450°F) for 15 minutes.

⇛ **Serve hot.**

BAKED PAV BHAJI (BAKED SPICY VEGETABLES ON TOAST)

The Indian pav bhaji covered with a Western sauce.

PREPARATION TIME : 15 MINUTES. COOKING TIME : 25 MINUTES. SERVES 6.

2 onions, finely chopped
4 tomatoes, finely chopped
2 teaspoons pav bhaji masala
$^3/_4$ teaspoon chilli powder
$^1/_4$ teaspoon turmeric powder
2 tablespoons chopped coriander
1 tablespoon finely chopped green chillies
2 teacups mixed boiled vegetables (french beans, carrots, green peas, cauliflower), chopped finely
2 potatoes, boiled and coarsely mashed
6 toast slices
4 tablespoons butter
salt to taste

For the topping
2 tablespoons beaten cream or 1 teacup white sauce
4 to 5 tablespoons grated cheese

1. Melt the butter on a tava (griddle) and fry the onions until slightly brown in colour.
2. Add the tomatoes, pav bhaji masala, chilli powder, turmeric powder, coriander and green chillies and fry for 4 to 5 minutes.
3. Add the mixed vegetables, potatoes and salt and cook for 2 to 3 minutes, sprinkling a little water from time to time.
4. Put the mixture in a baking dish, top with the beaten cream and cheese and bake in a hot oven at 200°C (400°F) for 10 to 15 minutes.

⇛ **Cut the toast in triangles, spread the mixture on top and serve hot.**

QUICK BABY CORN AND PANEER SUBZI

PICTURE ON PAGE 42

COLOURFUL AND EASY TO MAKE.

PREPARATION TIME: 10 MINUTES. COOKING TIME: 10 MINUTES. SERVES 4.

1 teacup sliced baby corn
1 teacup sliced paneer, page 72
1 teacup sliced onion
½ teacup sliced capsicum
1 teacup sliced tomatoes
1 teaspoon roasted cumin seed powder
½ teaspoon chilli powder
2 tablespoons oil
salt to taste

1. Heat the oil and fry the onion. Add the baby corn and capsicum and cook for at least 3 to 4 minutes.
2. Add the tomatoes and fry again.
3. Add the cumin seed powder, chilli powder and salt. Mix well and cook for 1 minute.
4. Add the paneer and cook for 3 minutes.

⇛ **Serve hot.**

Note: Parboil the baby corn if it is not tender.

JHAT-PAT BAINGAN SUBZI (FRIED AUBERGINES)

Even those who don't like baingans will love this dish.

PREPARATION TIME : 5 MINUTES. COOKING TIME : 5 MINUTES. SERVES 4.

250 grams baingan (aubergine), sliced crosswise
1/2 teaspoon mustard seeds
1 teaspoon sesame (til) seeds
1/2 teaspoon chilli powder
1/2 teaspoon turmeric powder
1 teaspoon gram flour (besan)
1/2 teaspoon sugar
1 tablespoon cashewnuts
5 to 6 raisins
2 tablespoons oil
salt to taste
oil for deep frying

1. Put the baingan slices in a colander, sprinkle with salt and leave aside for 15 minutes. Rinse thoroughly.
2. Heat the oil and fry the mustard seeds until they crackle. Add the sesame seeds, chilli powder, turmeric powder, gram flour, sugar, cashewnuts and raisins and fry for 1 minute.
3. Add the baingan and salt and cook for 1 to 2 minutes.

⇛ **Serve at once.**

STUFFED VEGETABLES

PICTURE ON PAGE 52

Gujarati style stuffed vegetables with crunchy powdered peanuts. You can use any combination of vegetables.

PREPARATION TIME : 10 MINUTES. COOKING TIME : 20 MINUTES. SERVES 6.

10 to 12 small potatoes
8 small brinjals
8 to 10 small onions
5 to 6 big green chillies (optional)

a pinch asafoetida
3 tablespoons oil

For the stuffing (to be made into a masala mixture)

1 teacup chopped coriander
$^1/_2$ grated fresh coconut
4 teaspoons coriander-cumin seed powder
2 teaspoons chilli powder
4 teaspoons sugar
1 teaspoon garam masala, page 70
$^1/_2$ teaspoon turmeric powder
3 tablespoons crushed roasted peanuts
salt to taste

1. Make a cross of 2 slits at right angles on the potatoes, brinjals and small onions.
2. Stuff the slits on the potatoes, brinjals and onions with the masala mixture.
3. Heat the oil in a broad vessel, add the asafoetida and fry for a few seconds.
4. Add the stuffed vegetables. Add $^1/_4$ cup of water and cook slowly until almost cooked.
5. Add the green chillies and cook for a few minutes.

⇛ **Serve hot.**

DHOKLA CORN SUBZI

PICTURE ON PAGE 52

A novel way for presenting vegetables.

PREPARATION TIME : 10 MINUTES. COOKING TIME : 30 MINUTES. SERVES 6.

2 teacups white dhoklas, cut into small pieces
2 teacups cooked tender corn
10 to 12 small potatoes, boiled
1 teaspoon cumin seeds
2 green chillies, chopped
$^1/_2$ teaspoon chopped ginger
4 large tomatoes
1 teaspoon chilli powder
a pinch sugar

salt to taste
4 tablespoons oil
oil for shallow frying

For the garnsish
chopped coriander

1. Put the tomatoes in boiling water for 10 minutes. Remove and blend into a purée.
2. Heat a little oil in a shallow frying pan, add the dhoklas and cook until slightly pink in colour. Remove.
3. Heat half of the oil and fry the potatoes. Remove and keep aside.
4. Heat the remaining oil in the frying pan and add the cumin seeds. When they crackle, add the green chillies and the ginger and fry for a few seconds. Add the tomato purée, the chilli powder, sugar and salt and cook for a few minutes.
5. Add the corn and potatoes and cook for a few minutes.

When you want to serve, serve hot topped with dhoklas and coriander.

MOONGFALI (GROUNDNUT) POTATO VEGETABLE

PICTURE ON PAGE 36

A nutritious, tasty vegetable.

PREPARATION TIME : 15 MINUTES. COOKING TIME : 20 MINUTES. SERVES 4.

1 teacup peanuts
3 potatoes, boiled
1 teaspoon sesame seeds
1 teaspoon cumin seeds
2 green chillies, finely chopped
a pinch asafoetida
3 curry leaves
a pinch sugar
2 teaspoons lemon juice
2 tablespoons oil
salt to taste

For the topping
chopped coriander

1. Soak the peanuts in water for 4 to 5 hours. Boil them until soft. Drain and keep aside.
2. Heat the oil and fry the sesame and cumin seeds until they crackle. Add the green chillies, asafoetida and curry leaves and fry for a few seconds.
3. Add the peanuts and fry again for a few minutes. Add the potatoes and sugar, mix well and fry. Add the salt and lemon juice and mix well.

⇛ **Serve hot topped with chopped coriander.**

TENDLI CASHEWNUT

A popular Manglorian vegetable.

PREPARATION TIME : 15 MINUTES. COOKING TIME : 15 MINUTES. SERVES 4.

2 teacups sliced tendlis
1/2 teacup cashewnuts
1/2 teaspoon mustard seeds
3 red chillies, broken into small pieces
a pinch sugar
2 tablespoons oil
salt to taste

For the topping
1/2 teacup grated coconut

1. Soak the cashewnuts in water for 4 to 5 hours. Boil for a few minutes until slightly tender. Drain and keep aside.
2. Heat the oil, add the mustard seeds and fry until they crackle. Add the chillies, tendlis and salt and fry for a while, sprinkling a little water while cooking.
3. Add the sugar, cover and cook until tender.
4. Add the cashewnuts, mix well and serve hot topped with grated coconut.

GANTHIA SUBZI

A popular Gujarati vegetable, made when fresh vegetables are not available.

PREPARATION TIME : 10 MINUTES. COOKING TIME : 10 MINUTES. SERVES 6.

3 teacups ganthia
$^1/_2$ teaspoon mustard seeds
$^1/_4$ teaspoon asafoetida
$^1/_4$ teaspoon turmeric powder
1 teaspoon chilli powder
1 teacup fresh curds
1 tablespoon chopped coriander
2 tablespoons oil
salt to taste

1. Heat the oil and fry the mustard seeds until they crackle.
2. Add the asafoetida, turmeric and chilli powders, curds and $^1/_2$ teacup of water and cook for a while. Add salt.
3. Just before serving, add the ganthia and give one boil.
4. Top with the coriander.

⇛ **Serve immediately.**

KAND, PANEER AND PEAS CHAAT

PICTURE ON PAGE 51

Chat-pata.

PREPARATION TIME : 30 MINUTES. COOKING TIME : 20 MINUTES. SERVES 6.

2 teacups kand pieces
2 teacups paneer cubes, page 72
2 teacups boiled peas
2 tablespoons cumin seeds
5 to 6 green chillies
25 mm. (1") ginger finely chopped
5 tablespoons oil
juice of 1 lemon

salt to taste
oil for frying

For the garnish
chopped coriander

1. Fry the kand pieces in hot oil until tender.
2. Fry the paneer pieces lightly.
3. Heat the oil in a pan and add the cumin seeds. When they crackle, add the green chillies and ginger and cook for a while.
4. Add the peas and cook for a while. Add the kand, paneer pieces, lemon juice and salt.

⇛ **Serve hot garnished with chopped coriander.**

BHINDI DAHI (KERALA STYLE)

PICTURE ON PAGE 36

South Indian style bhindi.

PREPARATION TIME : 20 MINUTES. COOKING TIME : 15 MINUTES. SERVES 6.

$^1/_2$ kg. bhindi (ladies fingers)
1 teaspoon cumin seeds
1 teaspoon mustard seeds
1 tablespoon urad dal
3 whole red chillies
5 to 6 curry leaves
1 onion, chopped
2 tomatoes, chopped
1 teaspoon chilli powder
$^1/_2$ teaspoon turmeric powder
$^1/_2$ teacup fresh curds
3 tablespoons oil
salt to taste
oil for deep frying

To be ground into a paste
1 coconut
2 tablespoon cashewnuts

For the bhindi
1. Cut the bhindi into 37 mm. ($1^1/_2$") pieces.
2. Deep fry in oil until crisp.
3. Heat the oil, add the cumin seeds, mustard seeds and urad dal and fry. After a while, add the red chillies and curry leaves and cook again until the seeds begin to crackle.
4. Add the onion and sauté until golden in colour.
5. Add the tomatoes, chilli powder, turmeric powder, the paste and salt and fry until the oil separates.
6. Add 1-1/4 cup of water to the curds and churn. Add to the mixture. Add the bhindi and cook for a few minutes.

⇛ **Serve hot.**

MIRCHI KA SALAN (HYDERABADI STYLE)

A popular Hyderabadi vegetable.

PREPARATION TIME : 20 MINUTES. COOKING TIME : 20 MINUTES. SERVES 6.

200 grams long green chillies
1 teaspoon cumin seeds
$^1/_2$ teaspoon mustard seeds
$^1/_4$ teaspoon fenugreek seeds
$^1/_4$ teaspoon onion seeds
6 curry leaves
$^1/_4$ teaspoon turmeric powder
2 tablespoons coriander-cumin seed powder
2 teaspoons chilli powder
4 tablespoons tamarind water, page 72
2 tablespoons chopped coriander
5 tablespoons oil
salt to taste

To be ground into a paste

6 cloves garlic
12 mm. (1/2") piece ginger
1 onion
2 tomatoes
3 tablespoons grated coconut

For the dry powder

2 tablespoons roasted peanuts
2 tablespoons sesame seeds
1 tablespoon cumin seeds

For the dry powder

1. Roast the peanuts, sesame seeds and cumin seeds lightly.
2. Remove and powder.

How to proceed

1. Heat the oil in a kadai.
2. Wash and slit the green chillies. Remove the seeds and fry in hot oil until they turn white. Remove.
3. In the same oil, add the cumin seeds, mustard seeds, fenugreek seeds, onion seeds and curry leaves. Cook until the seeds crackle.
4. Add the paste and fry for a while. Add the turmeric and coriander-cumin seed powder , chilli powder and dry powder masala. Cook for a few minutes until the oil comes on the top.
5. Add 2 cups of water and the tamarind water and cook until thick. Add the fried green chillies, coriander and salt and cook for a few minutes. The gravy should be thick.

⇛ **Serve hot.**

BASIC RECIPES

GARAM MASALA

200 grams cumin seeds
60 grams coriander seeds
50 grams cardamom
40 grams peppercorns
30 grams green cardamom
30 grams ginger
20 grams cinnamon
20 grams cloves
20 grams mace (javantri)
15 grams bay leaves
2 nutmegs
salt to taste

Warm all the ingredients lightly and make a fine powder or pound it. Use this in all your vegetables.

MAKHNI GRAVY

1 kg. tomatoes
1 tablespoon ginger-garlic paste
2 green chillies
10 cloves
8 cardamoms
100 grams butter
100 grams fresh cream
2 teaspoons powdered red chillies
$1^1/_2$ teaspoons kasuri methi (dried fenugreek leaves)
salt to taste

1. Cut the tomatoes. Add 3 cups of water, the ginger-garlic paste, green chillies, red chillies, cloves, cardamoms and salt. Cook on a slow flame until the mixture becomes like a sauce. Remove and strain.
2. Add the butter and cream and bring to a boil. If the gravy is sour, add a pinch of sugar or $^1/_2$ teaspoon honey.

3. Add the chilli powder, kasuri methi and salt and boil for 1 minute. Remove.

KADAI GRAVY

1 tablespoon coriander seeds
10 red chillies
750 grams tomatoes
4 green chillies
6 cloves garlic
50 mm. (2") piece ginger
1 teaspoon kasuri methi (dried fenugreek leaves)
1 teaspoon garam masala, page 70
4 tablespoons ghee
salt to taste

1. Roast the coriander seeds and red chillies lightly and pound.
2. Chop the tomatoes and green chillies.
3. Heat the ghee. Add the garlic and sauté over medium heat.
4. Add the pounded spices and cook for a few seconds. Add the green chillies and ginger and sauté for 30 seconds. Add the tomatoes and fry until the fat comes to the surface.
5. Add the kasuri methi and salt and sprinkle garam masala.

GREEN GRAVY

1 teacup chopped coriander
6 green chillies
12 mm. ($^1/_2$") piece ginger
1 onion
8 to 10 cloves garlic
$^1/_2$ teaspoon lemon juice
salt to taste

Grind the above ingredients into a paste with a little water.

WHITE GRAVY

2 medium onions
1 tablespoon cashewnut pieces
6 cloves garlic

12 mm. ($^1/_2$") piece ginger
3 cardamoms
2 cloves
1 bay leaf
2 green chillies, chopped
1 teacup fresh curds
1 tablespoon fresh cream
2 tablespoons ghee
salt to taste

1. Cut the onions into big pieces.
2. Add $^3/_4$ cup of water and boil. When cooked, add the cashewnut pieces, garlic and ginger. Remove and make a paste.
3. Heat the ghee and add the cardamoms, cloves and bay leaf and stir for $^1/_2$ minute. Add the onion-ginger paste and fry for 1 minute.
4. Add the green chillies and fry for a while. Remove from the heat.
5. Add the curds. Mix well and cook for $^1/_2$ minute, stirring continuously. Add the cream and salt.

PANEER

2 litres milk
juice of 2 lemons

1. Put the milk to boil. When it starts boiling, add the lemon juice. Remove from the heat and stir gently until the milk curdles and bluish water floats on top.
2. Strain. Tie the curdled milk in a muslin cloth and hang for at least 2 hours to allow the water to drain out.

⇛ **Use as required.**

TAMARIND WATER

50 grams tamarind (approximately 1 heaped tablespoon)

Soak the tamarind in $^1/_2$ teacup of water for $^1/_2$ hour. Squeeze out the tamarind water and discard the tamarind.